Woods,
A HARMONY

A collection of Poetry Classics – Vol 13

JANE SUMMERS

authorHOUSE®

AuthorHouse™
1663 Liberty Drive
Bloomington, IN 47403
www.authorhouse.com
Phone: 833-262-8899

Published by AuthorHouse 05/20/2023

ISBN: 979-8-8230-0844-0 (sc)
ISBN: 979-8-8230-0845-7 (e)

Contents

Acknowledgements.. ix

PART 1: POETRY CLASSICS

1. Words, Precious, A Value 1
2. Rocks, Crevices, A Mark!.. 2
3. Twigs, Not for a purpose!... 3
4. A Shadow, Only A Doubt! 4
5. A Tree Of Trust 5
6. A Banyan Tree, An Age, My Age I Realize!.............................. 6
7. A Leaf, A Grain, A Difference 8
8. Flowers, A Season, A Leaf, A Name 10
9. Twigs, Broken, A Story... 12
10. Weeds Amidst, Any!.. 13
11. Seeds, Several Colors, A Difference, A Fruit! 14
12. A Petal, A Pleat Less!...15
13. A style, A walk, A difference.. 16
14. A Smile, A Difference For A Success!................................... 18
15. A Sunrise Several Colors..19
16. Flowers, Leaves, A Fold! 20
17. Marigolds, Not A Carnation.. 21
18. Woods A Mystery.. 22
19. An art I blend!.. 23
20. A Lamp, I Use Everyday.. 24
21. Trees, An Art!... 25
22. A Sunflower Amidst, Roses!.. 26

23. A summer dance 27

24. Summer Nights! 28

25. A farmer, His days alone! 29

26. A farmer and his Cart! 30

27. A farm, poor! 31

28. A Village, Only A harmony 33

29. Leaves and Trees, Seasons 35

30. A day I wonder! 36

31. A conversation, My success! 37

32. An Ode, Only for a gratitude! 38

33. An Ode, My Harvest, A Festival! 39

34. A Mum, Not any this Spring! 41

35. Jasmines, My pearls, I count! 42

36. A Farmer, And His Home! (A Decor) 44

37. A Farmer, A Song, A Season 46

38. A farm, A farm Walk! 47

39. A village, A surprise! 49

40. A village, woods, A path home! 50

41. Woods, A flower, New! 51

42. Woods, A path, A bridge! 52

43. A harmony, a good! 53

44. A day, A walk, A village! 54

45. Marigolds, A seasonal Color! 55

46. My farm, 3, An acreage! 56

47. A farmer, And His Nine Grains! 57

48. A season, A conversation new! 58

49. Woods, A season, A Way! 59

50. A cottage, lost to time! 60

51. A home, A harmony! 61

52. A girl, lost to time! 62

53. A village, a friend, I need! 63

54. A friendship at sea! 64

55. An unknown Knoll! 65

56. An unknown tree for time! 67

57. My petals, a spring! 68

58. A tea kettle, My friend! 69

59. An autumn temple! 70

60. An autumn Fence, My tree! 71

61. An autumn Conversation! 72

62. A Summer dance!.. 73

63. A summer Leaf, A new Art!...74

64. A summer dress, A Rose My Pattern! 75

65. A winter, my sewing! 76

66. A winter, My blanket! 77

67. A leaf, a size, a measure!.. 78

68. A flower. A fragrance deep! 79

69. A Village Festival, A Ride My Pumpkin Cart!........ 80

70. A praise of a smile! 81

71. A song for an autumn season!................................... 82

72. A music, A Season!.. 83

73. A lace, a decor! 84

74. A Day Of Quiet 85

PART 2: MOVIE AUTUMN SACRED STILLS

Screenplay: Autumn Sacred Movie....................................... 89

PART 3: DURVUE VALUES

Peace And Harmony Values! 105

Acknowledgements

This book is dedicated to my father Dr. Chinta Chidananda Rao (Chief Medical Officer, South Central Railway), my mother Chinta Visalakshi, my husband Srinivas Madiraju, my daughter Anika Madiraju, my family and friends.

My sincere appreciation to all my friends, and well-wishers who have helped me at all times.

PART I

Poetry Classics

I. Words, Precious, A Value

Words spoken,
Is silver,
That will tarnish
Over time,
For no grace!
A brown,
A leaf,
A leaf, withered,
Wasted,
A life, An end,
Not remembered!
An autumn season!

Words
Precious,
Are
Actions spoken with grace,
Tis thewz
words bestowed!
A reward, true!

Memories,
Only remembered,
For an action, A grace!
A history,
A chapter,
Several chapters,
A book!

2. Rocks, Crevices, A Mark!

Rocks, Smooth, soft,
A shape,
A significance, A stone!
Rocks,
A crevice,
A shape, unknown, a size, a rock unknown!
Until,
A passage of time,
A shape, A color,
A season, A difference, a rock!
A mark I made!

3. Twigs, Not for a purpose!

Twigs broken
Fallen on the ground
Not a purpose!
Leaves a spring torn
A weather
Fallen on the ground
Not a purpose

A day
Only for something torn!
Several years a patch,
A tear not for a mend!
A sickness,
I did not live!
Not a purpose,
But a truth, true!
A memory cherished
By loved ones!

4. A Shadow, Only A Doubt?

A shadow,
An afternoon,
Not a reason to fault!

Several shadows,
An evening darkness,
Several a night,
I need to leave,
A hurry,
For a fault
Of me
Several!

A shadow,
I need to,
A sunlight,
A lamp
Until
A sunrise!

A wisdom,
I need to display,
A sunrise,
Only for a knowledge,
I need to learn!

A wisdom,
A learning,
A new autumn,
An autumn sacred
For new beginnings!

5. A Tree Of Trust

A maple tree,
A tree in
my front garden,
A tree of trust,
Day and night!
Days, only a green,
A conversation of a window, of topics!
Nights only a dark,
I look at my Conversations of Windows
Of a window, I learnt!
Maple, Seasons,
A learning, A knowledge!
Conversations Several,
Windows, many,
I learn!
A tree of trust
An adornment my front yard,
An age,
My home!

6. A Banyan Tree, An Age, My Age I Realize!

A banyan tree,
Several hundred years old,
A generation, several year old,
An age, I seek
My age,
For a conversation!
An age,
A wisdom,
I found!
An awakening,
My Knowledge!

A banyan tree,
A bench,
I sit,
Every!
Memories,
of knowledge I see!
I gather,
branches, and leaves,
A script,
A branch,
A leaf, true!

A wisdom,
A realization, true,
Every Season!

A banyan,
A wisdom,
I share!

7. A Leaf, A Grain, A Difference

A leaf,
A grain,
A difference,
A leaf,
I need to complement
A grain,
A meal,
I cook,
A supper!

A leaf,
A grain,
I use
To write,
A script,
A language
Unknown!
Words precious
For a meaning!

A leaf, a grain,
A harvest,
A season,
A difference,
A name!

Leaves,
Names,
Several,

Grains,
A few,
Only for a
Difference
Of a meal!

8. Flowers, A Season, A Leaf, A Name

Flowers of a season,
Mums, roses, Daisies,
A petal, A leaf,
A name new
A script,
my prayers,
New, unknown!

Flowers,
Of spring,
A name, new
A new year!
A petal, a leaf, my script, new!
A new year,
A name, new

Flowers,
Of summer,
Of a night,
of full moon!
A petal, a leaf,
A script,
Every,
A year!
A difference!
A Satyanarayana Vratam,
My prayers,
A difference,

A flower,
A shape,
A match,
A full moon!

9. Twigs, Broken, A Story

Twigs broken,
Several, a shape,
A shape,
Not a log!
A shape several,
Only a size
A difference, a log!

Twigs,
Thin, a decor,
A vase!
Cut, several pieces,
For a difference!
A twig,
Alone,
A purpose
Awry!

10. Weeds Amidst, Any!

Weeds, amidst, meadows green,
A weed,
I need to clear
For a meadow, not to fault!
Weeds, amidst,
An autumn season!
Weeds,
I do not know,
Only leaves, Brown,
I see,
Not any,
After
I clear,
A weed,
Unknown, an autumn season,
Only a leaf brown
Withered,
Several acres an Autumn!

11. Seeds, Several Colors, A Difference, A Fruit?

Tamarind seeds, a color, a brown,
Several shades, a brown,
Size, a difference,
A shape,
A tamarind!
A use,
A need,
For my soup!

A seed, a lemon
A color white,
A difference,
A color,
A difference, a size,
A tamarind,
A difference,
A fruit!

Seeds, fruits,
Many a color,
A difference,
A color,
A taste,
A fruit!

12. A Petal, A Pleat Less!

Petals,
A flower,
A petal less,
A skirt,
A style,
A difference,
A season!

Petals,
A season,
An autumn, a full,
Only for a
Petal thick,
A velvet,
A pleat,
A skirt,
Full!

A petal,
Not any a flower,
A hollow,
A cut,
A skirt,
Petals
Not any
For breeze!
Only a stem left,
A skirt!

13. A style, A walk, A difference

A style,
A walk A season,
A difference,
A dress,
A difference,
My size, a season!

A style,
A walk A difference,
Only a shoe,
For a glance!
A dress,
Only complete,
A style,
A shoe,
For a walk!

A style,
A grace,
An occassion,
A walk,
Head bent,
My look holy,
My walk,
To my temple!

A style,
A walk, a grace
An occassion,
I need to know,
For a walk!

14. A Smile, A Difference For A Success!

A smile,
Every, a day,
A morning,
Only for a success,
Of A day!

A smile,
Sincere,
To meet an eye,
A smile,
Only a Devotion
For a task!
A smile,
Of success,
To achieve
A sunset!

15. A Sunrise Several Colors

A sunrise,
Several colors,
A yellow,
A peace!
An orange,
A harmony!
A slight white,
A knowledge!
A blue,
A learning!
A red,
A tradition,
A green,
A custom!

Sunrise,
A blessing,
Everyday,
Only for a
Day of success!

16. Flowers, Leaves, A Fold?

Flowers, seasons,
A fold, A petal,
Inside,
Outside,
True,
A shape!

A leaf, a fold,
Only for an
Age, old!
Not a leaf new,
A straight!

Flowers, leaves,
A fold,
A difference,
A purpose,
Seasons!

Flowers, Leaves,
A harmony, seasons!
A color, seasons!
A harmony,
A need,
Every, a season!

17. Marigolds, Not A Carnation

Marigolds,
A color, yellow
A fragrance, an incense,
Not similar,
A carnation!
A difference,
A color,
A fragrance!
A shape,
A symmetry!

Marigolds,
A new,
Every Sankranti,
Festival,
A decoration,
My prayer room!

Marigolds,
A yellow,
Maroon,
A significance,
A kumkum,
Turmeric
A married lady!

18. Woods A Mystery

Woods,
A mystery,
Several new,
Trees,
Flowers,
Not any I know,
Similar, a village,
I do not know!

Woods,
Not A Mystery,
Last year!
A village,
I knew,
Flowers and trees,
I knew,
Oak and Maple,
Birch and Creepers
Daisies and lilies,
Roses and Mums!

Woods,
A Mystery,
I lost my path,
I chose a path,
I did not know,
I did not seek!

19. An art I blend?

An art I blend
Colors, I choose!
A gold bowl, to hold,
Purple grapes,
A green, a few pears,
Grape leaves, a twine,
My decor!
Peaches, and apples a few,
An outer decor,
A gold jug,
Amidst the decor!
Only a cover,
My grapevine leaves!

A background,
I need to blend!
A brown and a
Slight black,
My art,
My painting!
A background,
gold frame,
An ornate
My decor, A Vintage Frame,
To hold
My art!

20. A Lamp, I Use Everyday

A lamp. A need everyday!
A desk, a rest, my lamp!
A lamp I use,
For A learning, A work!
A day,
A night,
A lamp,
A part,
My room!

A lamp,
A golden yellow,
A light,
A shade green,
Only clear, a light!
I read, write,
Study!
A success,
Every,
My lamp,
My light, true!

21. Trees, An Art!

A summer,
An autumn,
Trees,
My art,
A background,
Pink and white, flowers
Peonies and dogwood,
A center,
My vase, a round,
A blue,
A few,
My yellow and blue
Primroses,
Only,
A few,
A branch!
A summer art tree,
Several,
A way,
I paint!
An art,
A conversation,
I learn from,
To arrange,
A vase,
A Window!

22. A Sunflower Amidst, Roses!

A sunflower, amiss, amidst, Several rose flowers!
Summer sunflowers, an art, I missed,
A centerpiece my garden!
Sunflowers,
A breeze, a summer!
A summer dance,
A learning!

Sunflowers seeds, I need a winter!
An arrangement, I clear,
I need to carve,
A new art!

A summer art,
I carve!
A rose art,
an art,
Of summer roses,
Colors, A blend!

A summer tea party, pink
A difference,
of a sunflower
Yellow art,
A summer lemon party,
A morning,
A difference,
Of a
Orange Art,
Of an autumn!

23. A summer dance

A summer dance, light,
A step, a skip,
A hand, a raise,
A swing,
Only for a summer
Carefree breeze!

A summer dance,
A reminder
Of summer memories,
A light hearted fun,
And laughter,
My summer dance,
Days of summer dreams,
An art,
A difference,
Every year!

24. Summer Nights!

Summer Nights,
A walk with friends light,
A step every, light
For a laughter,
Harmony a conversation!
Warm a sky of stars,
A comfort,
My friends!

Summer Nights,
Only for a song,
A song of peace
A song of comfort,
Family my health,
My summer nights
A rest, every summer!

Summer, days of friends,
Summer books, I read,
A summer night,
A dream, only happy!

25. A farmer, His days alone!

A farmer,
an age old,
Comfort,
An old chair,
A seat, a cushion!
Memories,
A smile!
Days of farming, only for a day of reminder!
A few crinkles, a smile!
A farm,
A weed, A plough,
A granary, a ready,
A farm ready!

My ole, wooden boxes,
I store, my farm treasures!
An occasional gold coin, I find!
A silver a rare!

A leaf, a birch silver, a shape!
My treasure box, I open
every autumn,
A treasure,
only to understand,
and finesse,
my conversation
For an autumn Harvest Festival!

26. A farmer and his Cart!

A farmer,
An autumn,
Only eager!

A cart,
I paint!
Tis, this autumn,
my autumn festival, a difference from last! My cart,
A new decor, A new art!
A decor yellow, red, a border,
A green, a hollow,
A center, a flower bunch!
A corner, a side, my grains!
Corns Vegetables, Fruits!

My
Autumn Cart,
a reminder,
of a home true!
A cart,
I only seek, everyday,
of an autumn festival,
To display,
My autumn harvest,
Only precious!

27. A farm, poor!

A farm poor,
this Spring,
A farm, abandoned,
Not any a person!
this farm!

Tis this village,
not any a harvest
or a supper meal!
A table empty!
Bread, corn, soups, Casseroles,
I miss!

It's afore,
Several years, ago,
a drought, still afresh
In the mind of the Villagers!

A village,
and villagers,
a look unkempt,
Torn and shabby clothes,
an apron,
not wiped,
This year!
My poor old farm,
Poor and empty,
Bare a room!

a good old kernel,
Oats,
Bread and butter,
A need!

A prayer
For a rain!
To keep my farm
And harvest true!

28. A Village, Only A harmony

Tis, Autumn time,
My village, A harmony,
Only for a celebration of Autumn festival!
Every home,
A pumpkin outside,
A porch,
A harmony, true!

Every home,
A supper meal,
A pumpkin soup,
A squash pickle,
A pecan,
A pumpkin pie, true!
A supper meal
Together,
Not a surprise, A family!
But a harmony,
Every family!

A village,
A decor,
Pine straw,
A scarecrow,
A symbol of harvest,
True,
A village corner,

Bicycles,
Vintage Cars,
A pride,
An autumn,
A Village Sacred!

29. Leaves and Trees, Seasons

Leaves and trees,
Seasons, Not similar!
A season, Autumn,
A tree, alone,
Leaves fallen,
Only for an autumn sacred,
For new beginnings,
Auspicious!

A spring,
A summer,
Leaves and trees,
A green and brown,
A harmony!
A breeze, A smile,
Of harmony

Swing,
My tree,
My leaves!
A summer, A calm,
An autumn,
A rest,
Old,
For New!

30. A day I wonder!

A day I wonder,
at my window!
A window,
of my studies,
A window of
My knowledge,
I gather,
From my studies,
A day true,
Trees, flowers,
I use
To relate my knowledge!

People outside my window, I seek,
To learn more,
An exchange of conversation,
A wisdom
A knowledge
I learn and seek!
A day of wonder true,
My knowledge, appreciated!
My conversation
of windows, true!

31. A conversation, My success!

A conversation,
I practice, everyday,
A conversation
Of a window,
A topic I choose!
A need to learn
And practice,
A success, mine!

Every season,
I celebrate,
My success,
A festival scared,
I bestow,
My gods,
Grains of rice
A blend of sugar and butter,
Fruits and flowers,
For a new learning
And success!

A conversation,
I train for a boundary
Of a topic,
A success,
Is a feedback
From
Every conversation!

32. An Ode, Only for a gratitude!

An ode,
I pray,
A gratitude,
For This autumn Season,
An autumn sacred true!
My harvest,
I realize this autumn!
A new learning!

A farm, to till, plough, seed,
A path new,
For a harvest, new!
My grains,
I store and clean,
Several bags to spare!
A harvest enough, For my family,
Every!

This autumn,
A spring
and Summer!
A prayer of gratitude
For the Spring harvest!

33. An Ode, My Harvest, A Festival?

An ode,
I sing,
A gratitude
of thee,
An autumn Harvest,
An autumn Sacred,
Only True,
This year!
A gratitude,
A sincerity,
A devotion
I bestow every day,
A farmer, poor, I am,
My prayers,
Only for a sincerity of a harvest to reap!
I learn, new, every,
To till a farm ,To reap!
Not a year,
I need to miss,
Every a year,
only
To appreciate and Celebrate!

A farmer, I am
I celebrate, my harvest!
A festival,
A gratitude, I bestow,
God!
A Supper every a table full, true!
A gratitude Bestowed
to a farmer
And his farm!

34. A Mum, Not any this Spring!

A farmer, every day,
A season, Spring, Summer, Autumn, Winter!
Only to sing!
A sunrise prayer,
A song
To bestow a gratitude,
To God!

A farmer,
An evening,
only to feel light hearted,
After a delicious supper!

Songs of a farm,
A note of,
A praise of a days work,
A prayer of harvest,
A song bestowed
For an autumn sacred,
A Celebration,
Only a joy,
A farmer, Joyous, happy,
For a pride of an autumn Harvest!
A harvest reaped, true!

35. Jasmines, My pearls, I count!

Jasmines,
A color one,
A white,
A cream
Jasmine stems,
Colors,
Several,
A green,
A orange,
A yellow,
A brown,
A color,
I choose of Jasmine to bestow God!

A color white,
An orange stem,
I cut every sunrise,
Place it in my
Silver flower bowl and handle,
To decorate my God, Lord Siva,
A name Parijatam, My jasmine!
Until An Autumn!

A color White,
A stem Green,
A decoration
Of my God, Lord Rama!
I bestow Jasmine, garlands!
A decoration my bun,
A decoration, a braid,
A bride,

Jasmines,
A fragrance,
A day,
A night,
A summer dream, true,
A summer fragrance,
Only a summer season,
I seek,
Every summer!

36. A Farmer, And His Home! (A Decor)

A farmer,
A decor,
A farm home,
A kitchen,
A living room,
An afternoon tea room,

A teapot,
A season,
A color,
A match, flowers and leaves,
A porcelain,
A teapot,
A Teacup, a rose!

A farm living room,
A formal
A match
A decor Cherry,
A coffee table
A decor,
A sofa!
A lamp a corner, an autumn!
A winter!

A breakfast Table, A spring!
A kitchen, A pink plaid, A tablecloth!
A pink, a yellow!
A tea pot,
A color pink
A match my Daisy cups, pink and white!

A farm home
A comfort,
A farmer and his family!

A sunset,
A blessing
A farmer and his family!
Every a season only a joy,
A farmer
And his family!

37. A Farmer, A Song, A Season

A farmer, every day,
A season, Spring, Summer, Autumn, Winter!
Only to sing!
A sunrise prayer,
A song
To bestow a gratitude,
To God!

A farmer,
An evening,
only to feel light hearted,
After a delicious supper!

Songs of a farm,
A note of,
A praise of a days work,
A prayer of harvest,
A song bestowed
For an autumn sacred,
A Celebration,
Only a joy,
A farmer, Joyous, happy,
For a pride of an autumn Harvest!
A harvest reaped, true!

38. A farm, A farm Walk!

A walk, my farm,
A farm,
Yellow, a corn,
Cornstalks, a color green,
Grains,
Several a color,
Brown, a white, a black,
Grains,
Rice, wheat, barley,
Vegetables,
Several colors,
A green, a yellow, an orange,
Peppers, beans, turnips, cabbages,
A walk, a weave,
Several acres,
A breeze,
My friend!
A summer!

A summer walk,
I count several acres,
An acre, a color, every,
Only for an arrangement!
A conversation,
To arrange,
My Acres,
A need!
A crop more,
A topic, new,
A crop different,

A season, new
A harvest,
A new study,
A different season!

39. A village, A surprise!

A village,
A surprise,
Every, a home,
Only to think
Alike,
A festival,
To celebrate
And share!

A decor,
Similar a home,
A color,
An arrangement,
Lights an arrangement,
A difference a home,
An autumn,
A winter,
Only for a difference
A spring, A summer,
A basket of
Diasies,
Roses,
Colors, bright,
A home!

40. A village, woods, A path home!

Woods, A village,
A path home, I traverse,
Every, a season, until,
A new,
A difference, a school,
New!

Woods,
A village, A path,
A season, A color, new!

41. Woods, A flower, New!

Woods, Flowers,
Many, A path,
Many, A Row!
A row,
A color,
A harmony!
A color,
Several rows,
A flower,
New,
A few!

Woods,
A flower, New,
A season!
A season, true!
A flower,
A way,
A form,
True!

42. Woods, A path, A bridge!

Woods,
Several paths,
A way
My home!
A path,
I won,
For a friendship!
An enemy,
I do not need any,
A friend to acquire,
A harmony!

Woods,
Several paths,
Not a need!
A path new,
Only for a difference,
A learning,
For a knowledge true!
A path to traverse,
Only wise!

43. A harmony, a good !

A harmony,
Every,
A peace,
All paths!

A harmony,
A mind,
Time,
Not
A disturbance,
Any,
All season!

Peace,
Only for
A laughter!
Peace only for a
Silence!
A quarrel,
Only
A disturbance,
Of peace!

44. A day, A walk, A village!

A day,
Only for a
Walk,
A season!

A walk
A conversation,
I walk,
Another!

A walk,
I learn, my steps,
A walk,
I see, new!
A walk,
Only for a
Harmony,
A mind!
Peace,
A sleep,
True!

45. Marigolds, A seasonal Color!

Marigolds,
Seasonal,
A color, New!

A color, a yellow,
A spring!
A color, a orange,
An autumn,
A color,
A Brown,
A winter!

Colors,
I learn
A tradition,
A custom,
A decoration,
Formal,
A festival!

46. My farm, 3, An acreage!

A farm,
Three,
An acreage,
A corn,
A rice,
A wheat!

Three,
A use,
A season,
A meal,
A home!

A grain,
A use,
A home,
Every,
A pick,
A use,
A season!

47. A farmer, And His Nine Grains!

A farm,
Nine grains,
Several Acres,
Not all acres,
A season!

An acre,
I spare,
A pumpkin,
An autumn,
An acre,
A sunflower,
An acre,
A cucumber
An acre
Only for a
Celebration,
An autumn festival,
For an
Autumn Auspicious!

48. A season, A conversation new!

A season, New,
A conversation,
New,
A renewal,
A need,
A continuity!

A conversation,
True,
A window,
A need!

A conversation,
Not for a harmony,
A conversation
Of a window,
Not an outcome,
For a Success!

A season,
A conversation,
A window,
True!

49. Woods, A season, A Way!

Woods,
A season,
A way,
A harmony, true!

Woods,
A season,
A color,
A shape,
A harmony true!

Woods,
A path,
I carve,
A harmony,
I need to carve,

A path of carve,
I need to
Change,
For a harmony,
A path!

50. A cottage, lost to time!

A cottage,
I did not visit, For time,
Lost,
Only, a few, Visitors,
A year!

A cottage, I passed by This year,
An autumn!
Lost to time, my cottage!
overgrown,
Bushes, Flowers, Lilies, roses,
not for any!

A silence only,
But For an autumn breeze,
Fallen leaves,
A sound soft,
A door,
An old bell, left alone For time!

Ivy,
A reminder, of a Conversation, of time,
A disquisition, I need to know!
A cottage,
Lost to time,
A reminder,
I need to visit only
For a renewal
Of an conversation,
A friendship to renew!

51. A home, A harmony!

A home,
A harmony, a winter,
Soft piano notes, my friend!
A friend,
A support
A harmony,
An evening!
A home,
My family!

A harmony,
A home,
A sunrise puja, Sacred,
An autumn!
A fragrance,
Sandalwood,
A Prasadam,
I bestow!
A Cheer,
A harmony
A mind!
A home!

52. A girl, lost to time!

A girl,

Lost to time,

A focus of her school,

Learning, A devotion!

Perseverance,

Focus,

A mind only for a success!

A girl,

Lost to time,

Days of conversations only for a Learning!

A conversation,

For a success!

A learning of

A mind, true!

53. A village, a friend, I need!

A village, new,
A friend,
I need,
A friend,
Only,
For a friendship,
A conversation,
A harmony,
Not to lose
A value,
Anytime!

A village, new,
A friend,
A need
For a
Harmony,
A culture,
I need to know,
For a
Conversation!
A harmony,
A village!

54. A friendship at sea!

A friendship,
Only a sail
Of a ship,
A friend at sea!
A friend,
A laughter,
Only,
An assent,
A wave!
A friend,
Only,
A walk,
A friendship,
I walk,
A color!
A color,
A sunrise,
Or
A color,
A sunset!

55. An unknown Knoll?

A knoll,
Unknown,
Far away,
A village!

A knoll,
I see faraway,
Flowers, tiny
a shape,
Star,
A shape round,
Colors
Yellow,
Purple,
A decor,
A side,
A knoll,
Only
For a
Count
Of
Stars!

A knoll,
A side,
A lake,
A sunrise,
A color,

Blue,
A night,
A gold!
A moon,
I see,
A night!

56. An unknown tree for time!

A tree, unknown for time!
A tree, unknown,
unless,
A path,
I walk,
To see
A tree!

A tree,
I see,
A season, a difference, a view!
An autumn, a purple,
Flowers, a breeze!
A summer, a pink, a, grace, a few!
I count, I pick,
A few,
I pass,
a tree!

57. My petals, a spring!

My petals, Several, a color, a flower,
A spring,
A white,
A pink!
An autumn,
A deep,
A dark,
A new art, every,
A flower,
A difference, a shade,
A color!

My dress,
A color, Several,
A spring,
A pink, a flower, small a white,
A vertical, line, a deep,
A few a, slant,
A big, round, a crepe,
A fall,
A few,
Folds, a grace!
Pleats, a spring, a style, true!

58. A tea kettle, My friend!

A tea kettle,
A sunrise,
A friend,
A tea,
Fragrance,
A leaf,
A teapot!

A color,
A white, a teapot
A match,
My tea,
A tea scone!
A cream,
A red!

A teacup,
A white,
Only,
Small!
A cup,
A size,
A measure,
My tea,
A sunrise!

59. An autumn temple!

An autumn temple Sacred,
Every an evening!
An afternoon,
I prepare,
A temple,
For an evening Darshanam!
A temple,
A prayer auspicious!
An Arti,
After,
A sound,
A bell,
Sacred!

A temple, I visit, an autumn,
A prayer, a peace, a mind, an autumn!
An autumn, auspicious, a day!
Blessings of God,
Of An Autumn Sacred!

60. An autumn Fence, My tree!

An autumn fence, I need an autumn,
For my vegetables, my flowers,
A kitchen garden!
An autumn fence, I need an autumn
For a meadow,
I grow,
A festival,
I celebrate,
an autumn!

An autumn fence, an autumn,
a color, auspicious,
I decorate,
an autumn fence!

An autumn fence,
A guard
A tulsi, My plant!
I worship, a tulsi, my goddess!
I pray, an autumn,
An autumn festival
A marriage of
My tulsi!

A tulsi,
I bestow, Kumkum, Turmeric, Flowers, necklace!
A prayer,
I chant,
an early sunrise!
A tulsi,
a prayer, a blessing, an autumn!

61. An autumn Conversation!

An autumn conversation,
A window,
I hold,
A season,
A day,
A topic,
A harmony!

A mind,
I traverse,
A way,
Back,
A flaw,
I change
For a value!

A mind
A value,
I instill,
A mindset,
A change,
A need!

A value,
A mindset,
Only,
A harmony,
A peace,
A value,
Any!

62. A Summer dance!

A summer dance,
A slight,
I skip,
A step I walk,
A step,
A right!
A step,
I run,
A step,
A left!

A summer dance,
A day,
Only,
For laughter!

A summer dance,
A night,
I walk,
A path,
A summer!

63. A summer Leaf, A new Art!

A summer leaf,
Several, a shape,
A shape,
A size,
A measure!

A shape,
A size,
A pleat,
A difference,
A leaf,
A measure!

A leaf,
A color,
A pleat,
A fabric,
A difference,
A measure,
A pleat!

64. A summer dress, A Rose My Pattern!

A rose,
A patchwork, my dress,
A rose patch pattern, several my quilt,
A rose,
a vase, a pattern!
My summer dress!

A rose
A color,
A pattern,
A way,
A path,
A grace,
A summer!

A summer dress light,
A breeze, slight, a step a dance,
A summer, a word, I replace,
A winter!

65. A winter, my sewing!

A winter,
A knitting,
A crotchet,
A comfort!
A sofa,
I lay,
a corner!
A cover, my blanket
For warmth!

A winter,
my winter velvets,
I decorate, a pattern!
my poinsettias a corner,
My toppings!

A winter, a sewing, I set aside,
a summer!
My sewing kit, a rest,
A dresser,
A winter,
A rest,
Only a summer!

66. A winter, My blanket?

A winter,
A blanket,
I sit,
A corner,
Only
To read,
A book,
An art,
I need,
A summer!

A winter,
A warmth,
Only,
A need,
A hearth,
A log,
A book,
My warmth!

67. A leaf, a size, a measure!

A leaf,
A size,
A measure!
A measure,
I need,
For my
Pleats!

A pleat,
Not a harmony,
My skirt,
A leaf,
A size,
A difference!

A leaf,
A pattern,
A color,
A leaf,
A measure,
My skirt!

68. A flower. A fragrance deep!

A flower,
A season,
A fragrance deep!
A mum,
A garland,
I bestow, My God !
A summer,
a rose, a fragrance, light,
A fragrance,
a conversation, a tea!
A spring!
A lily,
A fragrance, deep,
A breeze, a wave,
a lily, my skirt!
A spring,
A summer,
An autumn,
A season, a way!

69. A Village Festival, A Ride My Pumpkin Cart!

A village festival,
An autumn season,
My autumn cart, Laden,
With flowers, vegetables, Fruits,
My autumn cart, Colors,
I pick
From
A match of my autumn skirt!
An autumn cart, a season, autumn,
A feast,
an eye,
Every!

70. A praise of a smile!

A praise of a Smile, eyes,
A smile, Lips,
A gesture, Light hearted!
Sincere,
A smile!

A praise,
Of a smile,
an appreciation, of every!
A kindness, a gesture,
a grace, a harmony!
A smile,
Only sincere!

71. A song for an autumn season!

A song,

I write,

An autumn,

A note,

A line,

A breeze,

A note,

A line,

A wave,

A note,

A line,

A sound,

A song,

I wrap around,

A wrap,

A lyricone,

A song!

72. A music, A Season!

A music,
I play, Several days,
An autumn, a music,
I finesse!
A note,
A music,
I match!
A song,
A music,
A mind,
For new!
A song,
A conversation,
I understand, new!

73. A lace, a decor!

A lace,
A decor,
My handkerchief!
A lace,
A decor,
My quilt!
A lace,
a decor,
my slip!
A lace,
A difference,
A fabric,
A decor!
A lace, only,
For a decor formal!

74. A Day Of Quiet

A day of quiet,
A day,
Only,
For a
Prayer,
A kindness,
A mind,
A kindness,
My conversations,
A kindness,
My gestures,
A kindness,
I realized
After,
An
Unkind word!

PART II

Movie Autumn Sacred Stills

Screenplay: Autumn Sacred Movie

Autumn Sacred is based on the book Autumn Woods by Jane Summers.

Autumn Sacred is autumn auspicious and is sacred for new beginnings. (Some examples of autumn sacred are for new auspicious beginnings of an autumn (such as for a new education, a new marriage, a celebration of a new season, and others.)
Autumn is a way to build new stories of art, for new studies, new work activities, new knowledge acquisitions, and other new autumn activities.

The movie Autumn Sacred shows the different types of autumn values that happen, an autumn season.

Autumn notes are a way to remind one of autumn tasks and autumn prayers for fulfillment of an autumn sacred.

The film, Autumn Sacred brings autumn conversations to the screen. Autumn Conversations are based on the theme of Autumn Sacred. These are notes of Jane Summers!

Autumn Sacred consists of Lyriconnets, a two liner, autumnal song, a musical weave of autumnal poems and autumn songs of Jane Summers.

Autumn Sacred poems include values for friendship, grace, wisdom, promises, and devotion.

Scene1: Prayers of Peace
Offer flowers, milk and fruit to God on
Pooja thali.

Scene 2: Autumn Promises Song
A prayer offered to God at Sunrise. A song in praise of Autumn Season.
If the author is so meaningful, then that person must be a very peaceful
and beautiful person!

Scene 3: Autumn Ready - The last few warm days of summer
I remember the last few warm days of summer at my home. We would
make different types of spices for soups and vegetables, for an autumn,
autumn ready. We used cinnamon bark, a few types of lentils, coriander
and peppers for soups.

Scene 4: An autumn note
A note I penned today, I keep track of good tasks and good deeds to follow
every day. These are my ideal values for a life time.

Scene 5: Autumn Studies
An autumn note I wrote in the park. Read aloud a few lines. A song in
praise of Autumn Hills. An ode to Autumn Hills.

Scene 7: Autumn Reflection
An autumn reflection is a reflection I thought today of an autumn incident,
that happened a few years ago.

An autumn friendship is a branch of a tree extended in my window to me
for renewal of a friendship. I realized how strong the roots and branches
of a tree are, similar to a family.

A silence of a scenery is a way to understand and relate a scenery for
translation of a topic

Scene 8: An Autumn Success!

A brook, water still that only helped for a silence, a need for my studies to acquire knowledge. I was able to think calmly and understand the process and create it successfully.

A brook water, a small flow, only a flow in the right direction for not an overflow. A step in the right direction is only a path of success.

Scene 9 : Lyriconnets: 2 min

Buds I am a fold a sunrise, awake a few, flowers a sunset!

Autumn, a day of buds, and flowers,
Autumn a day of baskets and fruits
maize, wheat, corn, my only grains!
Days of autumn,
A smile, a return!

A return of a season
A Return of a celebration
A return of an autumn,
An Autumn Sacred!

Arranging a few buds and flowers and in a vase.

Scene 10: Lyriconnets: Freunde fur Tage

An Autumn Friendship, poem I read

Autumn gold,
My apples
A green,
A fragrance,
Sampengi!
A taste,
Afresh,
A fragrance,
A rose!

Autumn red,
My apples
A blend, a peach,
A deep purple rose!
Autumn red apples,
A fragrance,
A pomegranate!

My cheeks only
A blush,
My red apples,
Staring at me!
Shy,
Only, For a friendship!

Scene 11: Sunrise Scene

Prayers of Sunrise: Pray with the Pooja thali for blessings. Autumn Prayers, an autumn evening!

Scene12 : Autumn Leaves Poem

Fallen leaves, an autumn
Few days, a color yellow!
A yellow breeze, an autumn path,
A green, a yellow, a day,
A brown, a crisp, a reminder,
A life complete!
Until a Spring,
A New, True!

Lyriconnet
Fell a few,
A drizzle,
A pour,
A Day of autumn!

Scene 13: Autumn Art arrangement!

Location: Formal Living
Every, an Autumn,
An autumn art true!

Scene 14: Autumn Prayers Scene for Dasara festival
Lyriconnet:

Friends,
For days,
Friends, a few,
A Family for life!

Scene 15: Autumn Beads for fulfillment of an autumnal Value

Lyriconnet:
Dropped a few, To catch, an effort, a rain I save!

A Friday, I pray to Goddess Lakshmi for health, and Prosperity of every.

Scene 16: Autumn Auspicious

An autumn auspicious, I worship Goddess Durga on a full moon day. A few flowers I place before God and read my autumn prayers. An autumn prayer for health, cheer, success, and prosperity of a family

Scene 17: Autumn Memories

Flowers, several, a season,
A flower I choose,
A fragrance that lingers,
A memory, a season!
A Flower, A Season,
I choose,
A seasonal flower!

Lyriconnet: A song, a memory of a season!

Song, A sunrise,
Every,
A sunrise true!

Scene18: Autumn Promises

Autumn Promises,
A grace,
Every autumn!
Promises,
Only new, I add for a
season, new,
Promises
I renew,
An Autumn!

Scene19: Autumn Roses

Autumn Roses,
Colors of autumn,
Not a difference,
A summer!

Autumn Roses,
A Color, new,
My learning, new
A theme, new!

Lyriconnet:
Summers,
A season,
Summer
Colors
My smile!

Scene 20: Autumn Walk

Petals,
A grace,
A walk up and
Down, a step light!
Seasons, similar?
A summer true!
An autumn,
A coat, my dress,
My petals,
A walk steady,
Lest, a fall!
Winter, a walk
A firm step, true!

Petals, a sunrise true!
A walk true,
Seasons, a Walk true!

Scene 21:
Autumn Walk Song in the park

Scene 22: Autumn Corns

Autumn days,
My days busy,
My baskets always green, red and yellow!
My apples, plums!
My squashes, corns,
Never empty my farm!
My farm, a canvas
Of Autumn Colors!

Lyriconnets:
Autumn,
A sunset,

A match,
My autumn corns!

Scene 23: Autumn Gentle

Autumn gentle,
Every,
Any a season,
My autumn days,
Only happiness,
Smiles!
Peace,
Gentle,
A gesture,
Grace,
Beauty,
Walk,
An autumn gentle !

Lyriconnet:
For time you are a part of my life!

Scene 24: Autumn Togetherness

Time: 3 mins
An autumn
Sunrise
Sunset,
True
My togetherness, My Family!

A togetherness,
A harmony,
Every!
A difference any
Only for smiles, A togetherness!
My family

My support!

Lyriconnets

Sunrise, sunset,
An orange gold!
A few until a …

Scene25: Autumn Harmony

Days of autumn,
Sunrise, my flowers,
Flowers, smiles a harmony,
Autumn sunrise, time a harmony, smiles!

My autumn days,
Awaiting, a weave,
Smiles of sunset for a harmony!
Prayers of my autumn true!
A harmony of autumn smiles,
Flowers, sunset,
My skies, an orange
A harmony, smiles for
Autumn sunset time!

Lyriconnets

Scene 26: Autumn Devotion

Hills of Autumn Song - An ode to autumn hills

Autumn Hills,
Days of Autumn,
Prayers of an autumn auspicious,
Devotion, grace, trust, sincerity, loyalty,
Sacred an Autumn!
Holy, my prayers,

Trees, a harmony, a grace!
Hills, for time, a change of color!
Seasons, Autumn, A color true!

Scene 27: Autumn Auspicious

Autumn
Auspicious,
Prayers of Autumn,
For
Sincerity,
Loyalty,
Trust,
Devotion,
Appreciation,
Grace,
Respect,
Words I need
For A harmony,
My home,
My family,
Friends!

Scene 28: Autumn Sacred Song

A prayer, I remember a lifetime,
A grace, a season, an autumn, true!

Scene 29: Autumn Gratitude

Prayers of gratitude,
Every day,
A gratitude,
To my
Parents, teachers!

A gratitude,
For
Bestowing,
Family Values,
Education,
Other Values!

Blessings bestowed
Peace, A Harmony!

Autumn Sacred Song:
Home, a warmth, my family!
Togetherness, a harmony, a day,
Days of clouds, an art
Days of autumn, a color!
peace my living, A truth!

Scene 30: Autumn

Time:
Hills?
Dressed for an art?
My hills, a decoration, flowers, atop
Several trees a circle,
A dress for an evening, a yellow green, flowers, a circle!

Hills of winter,
A dress white, snow cap hills,
winter, a coat thick

Autumn Sacred Song:
Seasons, I remember your smile, every!
A face, a portrait, I cherish, a lifetime!
True seasons,
words, my songs
Songs a carve,
Art, my devotion, an autumn!

Bespoke autumn!
Truth an autumn!
Seasons an autumn!
An autumn, peace, my living, true!

PART III

Durvue Values

Peace And Harmony Values!

Harmony Values: Kindness, Gratitude, Sincerity!

Peace Values: Education, Knowledge, Devotion!

Family values of Harmony:
Support, Loyalty, Devotion, Trust, Discipline, Organization, Cleanliness!

Peach and harmony is a path
of progress and growth for success,
A mindset, a path of peace for a living!

Harmony is grace of words reserved, gestures reserved and silence reserved
to exude peace.

Durvue Flag:
A Gold Orange, A Silk Plain
A 4 corners, a flower, rose, a color red!
A center: A farm: grains, corns, vegetables, fruits and flowers!

A sunrise and sunset of a season. A prayer for a health, happiness, Prosperity
and Cheer!

Harmony values: a color, Light blue and white. a sky clear. No clouds for
harmony values to be met!

Peace Values:

Harmony values met and peace measured for progress and growth of success!

Emblem badge of Durvue
A round badge, in light white, a pink rose and a yellow daffodil, a harmony!

Peace and Harmony, We embody values of success!

Printed in the United States
by Baker & Taylor Publisher Services